TIME TO BE A TEEN

Your Circle of Friends

TIME TO BE A TEEN

Your Circle of Friends

**Claudine G. Wirths and
Mary Bowman-Kruhm
Cartoons by P. Stren**

Twenty-First Century Books

A Division of Henry Holt and Company
New York

Twenty-First Century Books
A Division of Henry Holt and Company, Inc.
115 West 18th Street
New York, NY 10011

Henry Holt® and colophon are trademarks of
Henry Holt and Company, Inc.
Publishers since 1866

Published in Canada by Fitzhenry & Whiteside Ltd.,
195 Allstate Parkway, Markham, Ontario L3R 4T8

Library of Congress Cataloging-in-Publication Data
Wirths, Claudine G.
      Your circle of friends / Claudine G. Wirths and Mary Bowman-Kruhm
   ; cartoons by Patti Stren.—1st ed.
         p.   cm.—(Time to be a teen)
      Includes index.
      Summary: Discusses in dialogue how to make and keep friends, and
   how friends can influence each other's lives.
      ISBN 0-8050-2073-X (alk. paper)
      1. Friendship—Juvenile literature. [1. Friendship.   2. Conduct
   of life.] I. Bowman-Kruhm, Mary.   II. Stren, Patti, ill.
   III. Title.   IV. Series.
   BF575.F66W57   1993
      158'.25—dc20
                                                    93-4752
                                                       CIP
                                                        AC

First Edition—1993

Printed in the United States of America
All first editions are printed on acid-free paper ∞.

10   9   8   7   6   5   4   3   2   1

To Scott Bradley Eargle
and Peter Clement
and Lynn Swanson

Claudine G. Wirths and
Mary Bowman-Kruhm

To my two best friends . . . my big brother David and
my husband Dr. Richard Cohen. "You're all I need to
reach for the stars."

P. Stren

Contents

INTRODUCTION
A Friend Indeed

"If you're really my friend, you won't ever tell . . ."
"Why should I like him just because his mom
is *your* friend?"
"I thought she was my friend, but was I ever wrong!"

Have you found that making and keeping friends isn't always easy? If so, this is a book that can help as you and your friendships grow and change.

When you were very little, your parents picked friends for you. Later you made friends with the kids in the neighborhood or in day-care. Even after you started school, you mostly chose friends from the kids that your parents knew or at least knew about.

As you get older, though, you meet a lot more kids from whom to choose your friends, ones that your parents don't even know. Although you want your parents to approve of them, you also want to choose friends who are just right for you.

In this book you'll think about how to make those friends, how to get along with them, and how to understand their influence on your life.

Sound good? Then join us while we talk with a young person a lot like you.

C.G.W.

M.B.-K.

1 Making Friends

Now that you are almost a teen, your world is changing. As your world grows to include people outside your family, friends are more important to you than when you were little. Friends may even seem like *the* most important people in your life.

I really envy kids when I hear a couple of them planning to get together after school. I had a really good friend, but the family moved away last summer. Now I'm left with nobody.

Have you tried to make friends with other kids?

Oh, I have friends. Let's say there's a big storm, and I'm stuck at school. I know several kids who would offer me a ride home. But that's not the kind of friend I'm talking about.

We know what you mean. When we talk about friendship, we think of having three circles of friends.

What do you mean by circles?

Pretend you are standing in the middle of the smallest circle in the drawing that follows—the one marked "C." The "C" in that circle stands for *closest*. The circle holds only you and your closest friend or friends, kids who are very special. Anyone in this circle is someone you trust to know things such as what your middle initial stands for and the person you really love! If you were stuck at school in a storm, they wouldn't leave until they knew you had a way home, too.

The slightly larger circle around the C circle is marked "H." "H" stands for the circle of friends with whom you *hang out*. These are people who share some of your interests and activities—the people on your team, in your club, in your religious group. You probably know all their names, first and last, and they know a little bit about you, but not your deep, dark secrets. Most of them would offer you a ride home if you got stuck at school.

The large circle marked "K" holds all the other people that you *know*. These are the rest of the kids in your classes, the kids of your parents' friends, students who may be a year or two older or younger. You may not even know their last names. They aren't strangers to you, but you don't know much about them, and they don't know much about you. If you saw them at the mall, you would say hi to them, and they would say hi back at you. They might or might not offer you a ride home if you were stuck at school.

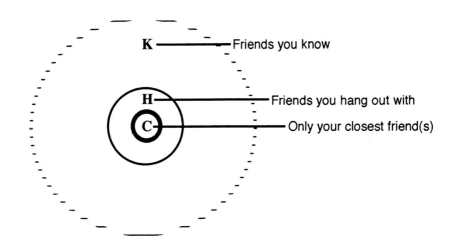

That's a cool way of looking at friends! Does everyone have the same size circles?

That's a good question. No, they don't. Everyone has different size circles. How outgoing the person is has a lot to do with the size of the circles. Some shy people have very small circles with very few friends in each circle.

They may not have anyone in the C circle. People who are very sociable may have several friends in the C circle, dozens in the H, and hundreds in the K.

Why did you draw breaks in the line around the K circle?

The K circle has a broken line to show that breaking into or out of a K circle is easy. If one of that group moves away, you may not notice for a few weeks that the person is gone.

The line around the H circle is solid because gaining or losing friends from an H circle is harder. Once those friends are made, they also tend to be around longer. You change them, but not so easily as the K ones. You may even go to a party for them if they move away, and you talk with your other friends about missing them.

The thick, solid line around the center circle says that bringing someone into the C circle or letting them out of it is hard. Finding a friend or friends to fit into your inner circle isn't easy, and losing them really hurts for a long time.

You said it. I really miss my friend who moved.
How do you spend your time now?

I fool around with my dog and play computer games. I guess I'm stuck being a loner.
If you really wanted to be with only your computer and dog, that would be okay. There's a lot to be said for

all types of relationships, human and nonhuman. Many kids go through times when they prefer to be mostly loners. But we hear you saying that you wish you had at least one close human friend.

You're right. The problem is that I talk to some other kids, but it isn't the same. Besides, I feel funny trying to make friends with someone new.

No one will ever take your friend's place for you, just as no one will ever take your place with your friend. But growing up means having the courage to look for new friends when you lose, or even outgrow, old ones.

I don't know how to go about finding a new close friend.

Trying to make a new close friend isn't easy, but you can do it if you work at it, are patient, and have a bit of luck. So let's talk about how you go about it. The process of adding to your circles of friends will be the same for you as for someone like your friend who moved to a strange town.

So do I start adding friends to my K circle first?

Right. To do that, you need to pay close attention to the kids who are around you. Study their faces and find names for the ones you never noticed before. Say a quiet hi when you pass them. Sit with different kids at lunch or offer to team up with different people in classes. Pretty soon you'll have a bunch of new friends in your K circle.

Then can I pick a new friend for my C circle?

No, not yet. Don't forget that you know little about kids in your K circle. You'll have the chance to get to know them when they slip into the H circle of kids you hang around with.

Does a close friend usually come from an H circle?

Yes, because they are the kids who dress and act like you and do things you also enjoy. To build your H circle of friends, consider what you like to do. Join clubs and groups of kids who share your interests.

How you get information about these groups depends in part on what kind of person you are. If you are shy, ask a teacher or the librarian how to get into one of the clubs, groups, or teams that appeals to you. If you aren't shy, ask some of the kids who are members how you can join.

Since you like computers and dogs, consider joining a computer user group or a kennel club.

Well, let's suppose I go to the computer club meeting. Once I get there, what should I do then?

You walk up to people and say, "Hi, my name is . . . What's yours?"

Who do I say that to?

People who aren't talking to someone else at that moment. Follow it up by telling them this is your first meeting. Then ask if they've been to a meeting before. If they have, ask what the group does. If they haven't, tell them that since you're new too, would they like to sit with you?

Okay. Let's say I've been to a few meetings of the computer club and have gotten to know some of the kids. What should I do next?

Pick one of the people who has shown that they like to talk with you or sit with you. Before that friend, who is now in your H circle, goes home after the meeting, make a specific plan. Do one of these:

- Invite the friend to come home with you and play games on your computer before the next meeting.
- Tell the friend you'd like to get together and ask for his or her phone number.
- Invite the person to go to a movie with you on the weekend.
- Suggest you walk your dogs along the same street.
- Offer to meet at your favorite fast-food place to get to know each other better.

But suppose I invite them and I don't like them that much when I get to know them better?

No problem. You aren't trying to make a C circle friend the first time, or even the second or third. You may have to invite a number of kids before you find one that you feel understands you and lets you be your real self. If you don't find any one person in the computer group that's quite right, join some other club. You might try the humane society, or a religious organization, or a community organization for kids outside of school. The important thing is to add to your H circle by making new friends who have like interests.

What should I do if I have trouble making even H friends in a club?

Some groups don't warm up to a new member easily. Knowing about talking in circles can help when you are the new kid:

- Remember that at first you are in everyone's K circle. If the group acts as if you don't exist, don't take it personally.
- Don't be too anxious; don't act crazy or do wild things to get attention.
- Watch the other kids to see how they talk and what they talk about. Hang around the edges of the group at first.
- Try to focus on the other kids and not have too much to say about yourself.

If you don't feel accepted after a couple of meetings, move on to another group.

If you still don't have any luck making friends, check with a favorite teacher or your counselor and ask how you might go about making friends more successfully. Your school may have a special group to help kids make friends. If the teacher says you are going about it the right way, just keep trying.

There's a new boy in my class. How do I get to be friends with him?

Say "Hi." Tell him your name and find out his. Ask what school he went to before and ask if you can help him get around. You don't have to pull him into your C circle; just help him into your H one by introducing him to your friends.

I'd like to get to know this girl in my class, too, but she's so shy, I'm not getting anywhere.

People who are born shy take time getting to know others. They have to know you very well before they let down their guard. However, once they make a friend, they tend to stay with that person, whereas some people who make friends quickly may drop them quickly.

Shy people can make friends more easily if they borrow tricks from those people who seem born knowing how to say the things that get other people interested. These friendly types operate like this:

- They are interested in other people and ask questions about what these people like and what they enjoy doing.
- They have a good sense of humor and can laugh at themselves when they make a mistake rather than get upset over it.

- They act sure of themselves even when they aren't.
- They share good stories about what they've seen or done. These stories help other people know them quickly.
- They take the first step and ask others to eat lunch with them or go to a movie. If the person turns them down, they go on to someone else.

My mom is the one who is afraid I'll be rejected! She asks other kids to come over to our house or gets their moms to invite me to theirs.

Relax and go along with your mom a time or two, and then tell her you would rather do it on your own. No matter how close you and your mom are, she can't know who will be just right as your friend. Taking charge of your social life is a big step on the road to growing up. Now that you are almost a teen, you need to find your own friends.

But to do most fun things, I have to ask Mom to drive us.

Asking a parent for help in carrying out a plan isn't the same as having a parent arrange everything. No problem with your mom driving you. The rest of the kids have to do the same thing.

Looks as though I need to get started if I'm going to begin filling up my circles of friends.

You're right. Just thinking and talking about making friends won't work. If you start spending time with kids who enjoy the same things you do, we bet that sooner or later you'll find a friend or maybe two that click with you. You'll invite them home. They'll invite you home, and before you know it, you will have a special someone in your C circle who is just right for you.

Then my problem will be how to keep them there. Let's talk about that.

2 Keeping a Friend

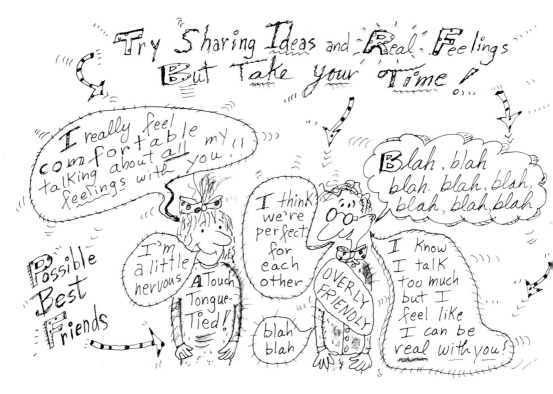

Well, do you still miss your old friend?

Not too much now, although sometimes I feel as if I'm not being loyal when I have such a good time with new friends.

Not only is it okay for you to move on to new friends, you *should* move on as soon as you can. By making new friends, you are saying that the old friend meant so much to you that you want to have the same kind of good feelings again. You wouldn't want your friend who moved to be missing you and never make any friends again, would you?

Not really. A part of me is sort of jealous that I'm not still my old friend's best friend, but when I stop and think about it, I know that we're both doing what we have to do by making new friends.

You are right. So tell me, how is your search for a close friend going?

I did as you said and joined the computer club. I've made a lot of H friends, and I think I've made a pretty good C friend there. We're beginning to have a lot of fun together.

That's great. You made a new friend pretty quickly. That doesn't always happen.

My new friend and I not only like a lot of the same things, but we're also always laughing at stuff.

So tell me more about your new friend.

We talk a lot, especially after school.

Good friends at your age talk to make sense out of their changing world. By talking to each other, you begin to see how you are alike and how you are different.

That's why I like sleeping over at my friend's house. My friend's parents let us talk and talk as long as we like. Next weekend we'll both stay at my house. I've got some great tapes that we want to play.

Sharing such things as your music and your ideas is an important part of a true C friendship. The more you get to know each other, the more you will know if your friendship is going to be close, especially if you talk about real feelings as well.

You do have to be careful, though. Don't share your closest feelings until you have known someone for many weeks. You may be tempted to tell too much about yourself in a late night sleepover when you feel close and warm. By the next day you could be sorry. Try out new friends on some small things of no special importance to find out if you can trust them to keep secrets and not to use what you shared to hurt you.

I already know I can trust this friend with a secret, but maybe I better check out another friend I've been hanging around with. This friend is kind of self-centered—eats the last piece of pizza, grabs the TV control and won't share it when we watch a show . . .

Why would you want to make friends with anyone like that?

Funny you should ask. My mom asked me the same thing. This kid is just different somehow, not like me. Knowing someone who doesn't care about being polite is kind of fun. We don't do anything really wrong, but I can tell that Mom doesn't like my friend.

Has she told you to stop seeing this friend?

No, but I think we'd better not spend time around my house. I don't want Mom to tell me I have to break it off.

There's nothing wrong with wanting to get along with all kinds of people. That's how you learn what you want in a friend and which friends are right for you. You also learn what your own values are.

Sooner or later almost everyone tries to make friends with someone who is very different. The kid who breaks rules, seems not to care what adults say, and lives for the moment can act like a magnet to the kind of person who generally follows the rules. In the same way a person who is good at sports seems like the perfect close friend to someone who prefers to paint and read in his or her spare time. Or a quiet only child wants to be close friends with someone who comes from a large, lively family.

You can be drawn to a person—either your own sex or the opposite—just *because* he or she is different. You wonder how it would feel to live that way. And the person can be drawn to you for the same reason. But usually you find out that you will not be lasting close friends. You find that you need a friend who likes many of the same things you do and behaves in the same way.

By not ordering you to break up with this friend, your mom is hoping that in the long run you'll make a good choice of friends.

Mom did say that if I get into trouble with this friend, she'll have a lot more to say. She's heard this kid is a troublemaker. She doesn't even want me to wear the same kind of clothes this kid wears. Sure, they aren't what I've been wearing, but they're just clothes.

Most parents step in if they feel that the safety or well-being of their child is at risk. That's part of the job of being a parent. Parents know that friends can have great power over one another. They hope that this power will be used in a good way. But they worry if a friend seems to have too much control over what their child wears, eats, says, and does.

If the two of you wear the same kind of clothes, your mom has a right to think you are being influenced. On the other hand, your friend's parents may be worried about the effect you are having on their child.

Do you mean they worry that I'll make their kid do bad things?

Parents may not say it just that way, but that's what they mean. It's important to spend some time with your friends' parents to let them know that you are polite and pleasant and willing to go along with the rules at their house, which may be very different from the rules at your house. Parents want their children to have friends they feel they can trust. So if you want to keep a friend, be sure not to betray the trust of the parents.

I'm not sure what you mean.

Keeping the trust of parents can be anything from getting back home on time when you go to the mall to not doing something really dumb like shoplifting. Parents hope that a friend will not get their child into trouble and, in fact, that the friend will keep their child out of it. Parents will nearly always blame the friend if a problem arises. The parents may insist that the friendship end.

I'd hate to lose my best friend the way my sister just did. A girl accused my sister of taking her sneakers. My sister laughed at her and called her a liar in front of some other kids. Now she won't speak to my sister.

Hmm. You raise a point about friendship that we need to talk about—what your sister could have done to prevent the trouble and what she could do to make friends again.

My sister says she doesn't care if they are friends again. The girl was always picking on her about how she cut her hair.

Many times when friends spend all their time together, small things about the other person can begin to break the friendship apart. To keep the friendship strong, your sister needed to make time to be with others and to be alone.

She could also have kept the fight from starting if she had respected the way the other girl felt. When the girl came up and said how angry she was, your sister should have been more careful about what she said.

Words have a lot of power. They can hurt people or help them, depending on what words are used. In this case, your sister made the girl even angrier by laughing at her and calling her a name.

I know she didn't mean to do that. I guess she'd better talk to some of the other kids and get them to talk to that girl.

Whoa. The problem is between your sister and the girl. Your sister needs to deal with her problem, not pass it off to someone else to handle. If your sister wants to make peace with her old friend, she's going to have to talk directly to her.

I don't know about my sister, but I think having anything to do with somebody after a fight is hard. I never know what to say.

Talking to that person is easier if you think about what you want to say ahead of time and practice saying it in front of a mirror.

I'd feel dumb talking to myself.

Actually, talking to yourself in the mirror is a good idea when you need to say something special to someone. Don't memorize what you are going to say, but go over in your mind what has happened and think about what you would like to say. Practice a few words using a low voice. Check out your expression when you speak to be sure it's a pleasant one. When you think you have the right approach, find a time when that person is alone and start talking. Remember to use cool words no matter what the other person says.

Cool words?

We mean cool in the old-fashioned sense of *not hot.* We mean not calling the person names or using swear words or insults.

Suppose the other person and I begin yelling at each other?

Try not to let what you say get to that point. But if you find yourself yelling, stop. Say you're getting so upset that you can't think straight, and because you'd like to be friends again, you'd rather talk about it later when both of you calm down. Name a time and place.

If you think you can't be in control, consider asking an adult you both like and trust to referee your meeting.

Oh, I don't think I'd actually start fighting with anyone.

Words can hurt as much as actual punches and be remembered long after a black eye or a hair pull is forgotten. Word fights can destroy friendship forever.

Isn't it easier just to forget about it when you have a fight with somebody and act as if nothing happened?

It is for the moment. But bad feelings don't usually

go away by themselves. Even though both parties try to be pleasant, the bad feelings are still there, and they can, and often do, build up and spill out at another time.

Suppose the other person stays mad even if I say I'm sorry?

That can happen; however, you'll know you've tried to make things right.

Close C circle friends don't *have* to fight, do they?

No, but to keep fights from starting, even the best friends need to work out everyday disagreements. What you do when you and a close friend have a disagreement depends in part on what you are like. Some friends like to shout at each other, but they must be careful not to use hot words. Other people need to talk quietly about a problem. Still others do better to write as a way of saying what is bothering them. No matter which way seems most comfortable to you, you always need to:

- Take time to be sure you know what the problem is.
- Think about what you might have done to cause the problem, as well as what your friend did. Admit your part in it.
- Be honest and up-front about what is bothering you. Start by saying, "When you . . . I feel . . ."
- Compromise whenever you can.
- Take turns giving in if compromise won't work.

Good friends are hard to find. Don't break up a friendship over something that won't really matter a month from now. Good friends agree to disagree on some things.

No chance of a disagreement today. My new friend from the computer club seemed worried about something. I'd better call and see what the story is.

That's what friendship is all about.

3 When a Friend Needs Help

One of the most important things friends do for you is to give you someone to talk with about your worries. You do the same for them.

I know what you mean. My friend and I have gotten used to talking over all the stuff that worries us—everything from schoolwork to haircuts.

How do you handle it when a friend comes to you with a problem?

Mostly I just listen.

Good for you. That's the single best thing you can do when friends are troubled. *Don't give advice—give only information* is a good rule.

What do you mean by that?

Most people don't really want advice. They need to solve their own problem. However, if the person needs information, you can provide the name of a person who will help them understand their problem. You might even give them the name of a book that would help them see their problem in a new way.

This time I may not be able to help. When I called, I found that my friend may have to go to the hospital. If that happens, I'd feel really weird about visiting.

Visiting a friend who is sick, either in the hospital or at home, is a special part of friendship. Dealing with it takes a little courage. Remember that you want to help the other person. The less you think about yourself, the more at ease you will feel. Here are some suggestions:

- If you haven't been around a hospital, walk a bit in the hall and get used to the sounds, sights, and smells so you won't look upset when you visit your friend.
- Don't be shocked if you find that your friend may not look well and may be hooked up to all kinds of gadgets.
- Take along a small gift. No food, even if your friend asks for it. Many patients are on strict diets, and

the wrong food can make them worse. Better to take a puzzle, game, or magazine.

- Take your cues from your friend. If you don't know whether it is okay to do something such as sit on the bed, ask.
- Relax and have some quiet fun. Remember, the person who is sick is your *friend*. That hasn't changed.

I guess I could do those things. From what my friend told me, everything will be okay. But I get really scared at the thought that a close friend could die. No one close to me has ever died, and I wonder how I would feel.

We're glad your friend will probably be okay. Most people worry about the worst happening, however, just like you, so let's talk about it.

When a friend dies, you go through many different feelings. At first you say, "No way. This can't happen." Gradually you understand that it did, and you become sad. This grieving will last a while. To deal with your sadness, draw pictures, send notes to the loved ones of the person who died, write a poem. Don't let anyone tell you that you shouldn't grieve. You have a right to be sad.

Most of all, find a grown-up friend to talk to about death and dying and your friend who died. Call a hotline if you don't know anyone. You can find hotlines listed in the front of the telephone book under community service numbers or call the operator. Ask any questions you have. If you are angry about anything, say so. If you feel guilty or responsible in some way, tell the person. If you have fears, share them. These are natural feelings, and you need to talk about them.

I never thought of talking to someone about death.

Talking to someone who can help you is good advice whenever you face a serious problem. No matter what has happened to you or what you may have done, never ever let yourself feel so blue that you decide life isn't worth living. Time will heal your worst hurts if you share with someone who cares. And there are people who do. *Find them!*

This has been an awful week. In social studies class we're studying about why a lot of girls want to look thin and guys try to look muscled. After class, a girl I know pretty well—she's in my H circle—told me a secret. She said she does the bit about eating a lot of junk food and then throwing up. I didn't know what to say or do for her.

Be up front in a case like that. Say, "You sound to me like you've got a real problem. Tell your mom you need some help. You're fooling around with your life, and I don't want you to do that." Make her know what she's doing is serious.

She said a lot of other stuff. One of the things she said was that she's mad at her mom.

Then the next best thing is to find her favorite teacher, a counselor, a nurse if your school has one, or an adult friend. Quietly go to that adult and tell them. Let them know you have been told the information as a secret but that you are worried because she needs more help than you can give.

But aren't friends supposed to keep a secret?

A friend should tell a secret *if* it involves another person's well-being and if that person clearly needs more help than a friend can give.

Suppose the girl tells me another "secret"—she and her mom are getting some help from a counselor . . . ?

That is a secret you would keep. At that point you can be a good friend by listening and supporting what she is doing to solve her problem.

I wish she would get help. I sure don't want her mad at me for telling.

If she does not seem to be dealing with her problem, better that she be mad at you for telling than for you to let her get deeper and deeper into trouble. That goes for telling on anyone who lets you know their "secret" if that secret concerns their health and perhaps even their life.

Do people let someone in on a "secret" as a way of asking for help?

Secretly telling someone is often a call for help. If a person is in very deep trouble, he or she may not talk about it at all, but the person's behavior changes. Because the person doesn't talk about the trouble, only a close friend may notice. Another way people let someone know they need help is by bragging about what they are doing.

I should tell my brother that. He has a friend who stole a camcorder and then sold it for $200. The police caught him. Now he's bragging about being caught.

His bragging may be a way of asking for help. But people brag for other reasons. He may have very different values from your brother and feel that being arrested is a sign of manhood. Or he may be embarrassed, and his bragging is a way of covering his embarrassment.

All the kids are asking my brother what it's like to have a jailbird for a good friend.

When a good friend (or someone in your family) makes a serious mistake and does something very bad, friends and loved ones are bound to feel mixed up and confused and sad.

Yeah, my brother doesn't know what to say. He still wants to be friends, but he doesn't want his friend to

think he believes stealing is okay. Our parents don't want my brother even to talk to him for fear people will think he's a thief, too.

Almost everyone has done something really wrong at least once in his or her life. Most people figure out right away that it isn't smart to do something like that again. If your brother's friend has had a clean record up until now, admits he was wrong, pays back the money, and accepts his punishment, he is probably a pretty good guy.

Do you think it's okay for my brother to hang around with him?

Your brother will have to go with what your parents say, of course. But if he truly has reason to believe this was a one-time thing, he should stick by his friend.

What should I say when other kids bad-mouth him?

When you're in a crowd, you probably can't help him by defending him. Don't say anything. If you are with only one or two other people, ask them if they've been so goody-goody that they can afford to make fun of someone else. Then drop it. Talk will be big for a little while, then something else will happen, and people will forget all about the old story and talk about the new one.

I came close to being the one talked about not long ago. I went to the mall to see a TV star. The crowd pushed so hard to get close to the stage that two kids next to me got stepped on, and their legs were broken.

I wish I had been the one to break my leg. The story was all over the evening TV news. The star went to see them in the hospital and gave them autographs and everything.

You must really like that star to be willing to get your leg broken. Can we talk about that?

4 Special Friends

Do you think being friends with a TV or movie actor, a musician, or a sports hero would be fun? Many young people who are almost teens surely do. They dream of having their favorites in their C and H circles. They dream of living the kind of life they lead and maybe being a star themselves.

I don't dream I could be a star, but I have thought about how cool it would be to hang out with some of them. They seem as if they would be a lot more fun than the kids around here.

You used the right word—*seem*. The truth is that what you read in fan magazines about these stars is mostly made up. The person you see on screen or on stage is a pretend person. If you really got to know that star, you would find that person no more and no less fun than your own friends.

Well . . . maybe so. Are you saying I'm crazy if I think about being friends with a rock star?

No, we aren't saying that you're crazy. Daydreaming can help you escape the humdrum and even the stress and problems of everyday life. But ask yourself if you spend too much time daydreaming about a make-believe life:

- Is your make-believe life more important than the real world?
- Does a fantasy friend keep you from making a real-life close friend?
- Do you daydream when you have jobs around the house or schoolwork you should be doing?
- Do you daydream away a lot of the day to escape from a major problem in your life?
- Is the fantasy friend beginning to seem more and more like a real friend?

A "yes" answer to any of these questions is a warning sign that you need to talk to someone you trust, someone who can help you sort out your real world from your fantasy world.

But I like having pictures of my favorites on my wall. I even belong to a fan club.

There's nothing wrong with that. Actors, musicians, and athletes like to get fan mail, and even if they don't personally answer your letter, they will usually send you a picture. Have fun being a fan. But don't get so carried away by wanting to get close to the star that you try to go backstage or sneak into hotel rooms. You will only run into trouble, and you'll make the star very angry.

Stars off-camera and off-stage are often much older and very different from what they seem.

I wouldn't mind if they were older. Lots of kids my age like older friends. One girl I know says she is in love with the phys. ed. teacher. He's married, but she has the idea that he secretly loves her.

Many almost-teens go through a kind of "falling in love" with a grown-up. Just like the girl you know, you may find yourself feeling in love with an older someone— a teacher, an adult friend, or friends of older brothers and sisters. If you use that feeling to help you do well in school or do better on the team so that special person will notice you, that's fine. *Stop there.* Don't try to persuade yourself that the person loves you. And don't try to get the older person to fall in love with you. Settle for "like" rather than "love." Carrying the special feeling you have for that person any further is a big mistake.

Is it all right to tell the person that you feel, uh, kind of special about them?

As long as you say it just that way. But don't say you love him or her. And don't try to be alone with the person. Most grown-ups know how to handle what they call a "crush." Some don't, however, and you could be badly hurt, either by their rejection or their taking advantage of you. Protect yourself and your friend by keeping "love" feelings a secret. If you have to share your feelings, share them only with a close C circle friend, one who can keep a secret. In time, you'll shift this growing-up kind of love to someone your own age, and the older person won't matter so much to you.

How old is too old for me?

Experience has shown that at your age you'll have the best time with people no more than a grade above or a grade below you. If you find that your only friends are two or more grades ahead or behind you, think about talking to a counselor. Having only younger friends says you may need some help accepting yourself. Having only older friends can get you into experiences you aren't physically and emotionally ready for.

You talk about falling in love. Can't I just be friends with someone of the opposite sex?

Oh, for sure. Many boys say they know a special girl that they think of as a close C friend, and many girls will say they have a C friend who is a boy, but not a boyfriend. These are often kids who have known one another for many years. At your age they usually keep this special friend sort of secret. For example, they may celebrate each other's birthdays the day before the big same-sex party. However, they often turn to each other when they have problems, especially girlfriend or boyfriend ones, and they also often share a favorite hobby or sport. They are truly just friends, and they are not having a boyfriend/girlfriend relationship.

Why do some parents act real uptight about boy and girl friendships?

Adults have learned the hard way that sometimes when you least expect it, a boy and girl friendship can become a boyfriend/girlfriend relationship. So when adults see a boy and a girl going off hiking alone or spending time in each other's rooms, they begin to worry about their having sex.

The best policy is to behave in such a way that you give the grown-ups nothing to worry about. You can be alone together, but leave the door open. Go hiking, but don't camp overnight except with a group. Above all, don't spend more of your time with a girlfriend or boyfriend than you do with friends of your own sex or with a crowd that includes both boys and girls.

Suppose your friend wants to change from being a friend to a boyfriend or girlfriend and you don't want to?

First, you have to be very careful what you say. Because you have been close friends, you may feel you must go along with the other person. If you don't honestly want to, say so. Say as kindly as you can, "I'd rather stay just friends. I'm not ready for anything more." Don't be hurt, however, if the other person prefers not to be friends at all. He or she may feel embarrassed or regard what you said as a put-down, no matter how much you tried not to hurt the other person. He or she may feel ready for a real date and doesn't want just to do things together. Whatever the reason, accept the other person's feelings but don't change your mind.

My parents kid about not letting me date until I'm twenty-five!

Your parents are joking, but they are also telling you they are concerned about your having a boyfriend/girlfriend relationship. They are concerned about your having sex too early.

We tease the kids who are going steady, but I don't see what the big deal is if they send each other notes in math or hold hands walking around the mall. That sure isn't hot sex like on TV.

Sending notes (unless the teacher catches you and you get detention) or holding hands is no big deal. But two people deciding they are ready emotionally and physically for a relationship *is* a big deal.

We've talked about feelings that come about when

you have a close friend. Any time friendship changes to boyfriend/girlfriend, feelings go up and down like a high-speed yo-yo. Here's a real-life math problem for you: Multiply your feelings by 100 when you have a relationship with someone of the opposite sex. Then add in the physical part of the problem.

And finally, keep in mind that a boy/girl relationship can get complicated and crazy. The pluses of having a boyfriend or girlfriend are good feelings and fun. There are minuses, too. One is the time it takes (maybe time from friendships with other friends). Another can be the bad feelings when problems come up, as they surely will. Ask yourself if you're ready to solve this kind of problem.

I don't think so, at least right now. Last week at a party a couple of kids talked everyone into playing a kissing game. It was fun at first, but it went on and on. The jokes and other things some kids said got embarrassing. Some of us felt sort of dumb, but we couldn't figure how to get out of it.

Whether you are almost a teen or any other age, *never* go along with sexual activity of any kind—not even hand-holding—that you aren't absolutely, positively sure you want. *Your body belongs to you.* Even your closest friend has no right to pressure you to take any risks with it. (Nor do you have any right to pressure anyone else to take risks.)

We admit, though, making a choice whether or not

to go along with the others in a group is a tough problem. If several of you felt "dumb," you might talk with one another ahead of time about what you'll do if the same happens at the next party.

The girl and boy who started that kissing game walk around holding hands and acting as though they are in love. Behind his back, though, she makes fun of him. We think she just goes out with him because he has lots of money to spend on her.

Short-term friends of either sex can sometimes be bought with money and gifts. Most of us find it easy to overlook someone's faults if we are being treated to super parties and great presents. Nevertheless, in time, friendships based on money and presents fall apart. You can't buy a true friend.

Some young people find out the hard way that buying friends doesn't work. If they get into trouble, they soon find out that their bought "friends" leave them. Only true friends stick by you in good times and bad, rich or poor. True friends like you for who you are, not your money or what you can do for them.

I know. My best friend always forgets to take money, and I have to make a loan.

Be careful about friends and money. Never loan a friend more money than you can afford to lose. Even the best friend sometimes forgets or can't pay back a loan. That can make a real dent in a friendship. The best policy is never to lend or borrow more than a couple of dollars and never lend or borrow any more until that is paid back.

When a bunch of us go to the fast-food place, a couple of the kids never have any money. Instead of anyone having to borrow, those of us with money put what we have on the table, divide it up, and buy something to eat for everybody. I think that's real friendship.

So do we. But not all groups work as smoothly for everybody's welfare as your group seems to do. So let's talk about what can happen when your best friend is a bunch of friends.

5 In-Groups and Other Groups

The need to belong seems to be part of each of us. Belonging to a group gives us an identity. It tells the world who we are. Our H friends often come from groups to which we belong.

Yeah, I like belonging to the computer club. Even some parents and teachers are really impressed. They act as if belonging to a computer club is a big deal.

As you have found, belonging to a group gives people greater influence and strength than they have alone. If you want that influence and strength to be positive, as with the computer club, pick the groups you belong to very carefully. This is a good time to remember the old saying, "Be careful what you wish for; you might get it."

I don't understand why you say that.

Getting out of most groups is harder than getting in. When you are in a group, you hate to admit you made a mistake, so once you join, you stay. Before you join a group, find out what the group is all about.

- Who really runs it?
- What must you do to get along with group members?
- What must you do to stay in the group?
- What kind of people become leaders? Can you become a leader if you want to? If so, how?
- What do people you respect think about the group?
- Would you be embarrassed to tell your mom how you act when you are in the group?

Thinking about the answers to these questions can save you from having problems later, after you join the group.

I don't have to think about those questions. The computer club is the only group I belong to.

Ah, but the most important groups outside your family may not be clubs and other organized groups with officers and a set meeting time and place. Now that you are almost a teen, you will find more and more informal groups that you might join. They are made up of kids who are interested in the same things, like kids in your neighborhood who get together to play ball.

Most of these groups accept you as a member if you are friendly to them and have a like interest. Sometimes, however, a group sets itself up as social snobs, kids who choose who's cool and allow only those they want to join.

I know what you mean. There are four girls and four guys in our school who think they are so special. They act as if they're better than anyone else. They make me mad, and yet sometimes I wish I could hang out with them.

Why do you wish you could hang out with them?

Because they almost run the school.

Are you saying that belonging to the in-group gives the members of it more power and privileges than belonging to any other group around the school?

They have a lot of power and privileges. They push other people around in rest rooms and save places for one another in the cafeteria line when they aren't supposed to. Even the teachers seem to treat them differently.

That happens. Some teachers may be influenced by students who are popular. So no wonder that, at your age, you and almost every other kid in the school want to belong to the in-group. That's why many students copy the clothes or the fads or the sayings of those students. They hope that other people will at least not think they are in the out-group.

But besides wishing you belonged to the in-group, don't you also wish you had a million dollars?

Sure, but what does that have to do with the in-group?

You want some things in life that you won't get. If you let yourself, you can be miserable all your teen years, wishing you had tons of money or belonged to the in-group. On the other hand, if you work at being a happy and successful person, you can find your own group without ever being rich or belonging to the in-group.

The computer club that I belong to seems dull when I see those in-crowd kids at lunch in their great-looking clothes, sitting around together and laughing and having fun.

What do they do to have fun at lunch?

Mostly a couple of them start picking on some kid who may walk funny or act dumb. The others all giggle and laugh and go along with it.

Would you want other people to think of you as the kind of person who laughs at people who are different?

Not really.

That's the dark side of belonging to a group. When

you are in a group, you tend to follow the leader. The more important the group is to you, the less likely you are to question what the leader does or says. The truth is that some members of the in-group at your school are afraid they won't keep their spot in the group. To be a member, they do and say things under pressure from the leaders that they would never do and say on their own.

Something like that has just happened in the computer club, and I don't know what to do. The other day when we opened up a computer, we found that the math teacher had left his file of math tests. One kid started laughing and talking about printing off copies and selling them. I think we'd have done it, too, but our teacher-adviser came in. We pretended we were talking about something else. Monday when the club meets, I know that same kid will want to check out those tests again.

What do you think you should do?

I know it's wrong and we shouldn't do it, but . . .

That's what we meant when we spoke about the dark side of belonging to a group. You make it clear to us that you wouldn't do it if you were alone. Because belonging to the group means so much to you, you are tempted to go along with it. Is that about right?

I'm afraid so.

Feeling tempted is okay. You're normal for feeling that way. But giving in to the temptation is another matter. As you become a teen, you will be faced with making more choices than when you were a little kid. Will you be an independent, confident person who makes choices based on personal values? Or a person who lets other people control your life? If you just go along with others, you are choosing to let them choose for you.

I don't understand.

When you have the chance to choose and you let friends choose for you, you are still making a choice. Don't just go along with the others. *You* make the choice. Take charge of your life.

You mean I have to tell the computer club members not to do it?

Only you can decide what you will do. You know what your values are. In this situation you have several choices besides just going along with the others:

- You can stay away from the next meeting.
- You can go to the meeting and not say anything.
- You can tell the others that it is illegal and wrong and that you won't do it and then leave.
- You can tell the others that if they do it, you will tell the teacher-adviser.
- You can call the teacher-adviser over the weekend and tell him what's up.

Oh, gee. You don't make my decision any easier. I never thought of all those different ways of handling it.

You always have choices. Some choices are easy to make. You like chocolate marshmallow, so you don't look at all the other flavors.

Some are harder choices that are not quite so easy to make. You want to take music lessons, but you have just been picked for the tennis team.

Some choices are hard to make, and you have to think long and carefully to decide. How to handle the computer club problem is a hard choice.

I have a tough time making choices. I don't always know how to choose.

There are basically only three ways to make choices:

- Choose what seems right at the time. Don't sweat the little choices.
- Make most harder choices by thinking about how your choice will affect you. If you choose A, will your choice get you in trouble? If you choose B, will you feel good about yourself? If you choose C, will you help a friend and not hurt yourself? When you make harder choices, stop and think about the consequences to you and others.
- Make *very* hard choices by taking time to study each option. You may want to use a chart and write down the pros and cons of each choice, and the possible outcomes. Take your time deciding, and don't let others rush you when a choice is really important to you.

But sometimes hard choices have to be made in a hurry. If the teacher-adviser hadn't walked in at the computer club meeting, I'd have had to decide what to do right then. I wouldn't have had time to write down pros and cons.

One smart thing you can do is think through a lot of hard choices (like smoking versus not smoking) when you have plenty of time to study the consequences. Make up your mind beforehand, and then, when you find yourself having to make a hard choice quickly, you'll already know what you want to do.

New problems, like the one with the computer club, will always come up, however. When you have to make an unexpected choice in a hurry, picture in your mind an adult you respect—your mom, dad, aunt, or favorite teacher. What would that person tell you to do? Use this as a quick check on whether your choice is the right one.

I'm not sure that will work when I'm having a great time with friends and they want me to do something I don't want to do.

What do you do now when you get that funny feeling in your stomach that says your friends aren't making a choice that's right for you?

I just kind of ignore the feeling and go along with them. But I know I shouldn't.

Slip off to the rest room or telephone or anywhere away from the crowd for a minute. If you can't physically get away from the others, close your eyes and try not to listen to what's going on. Think about why your stomach is feeling funny. Think about what your choices are in this situation. If you feel sure that staying with the crowd will push you to make a choice you'll regret later, leave.

Won't the rest of the kids be mad at me for not going along with them?

For the moment, they probably will. They may call you names or make fun of you to try to keep you with them.

But I don't want my friends mad at me.

More and more often as you become a teen, you will have to decide for yourself. Much of the time you will agree with your friends, but sometimes you will feel they are making a poor choice.

I guess I had better choose my friends, both close C friends and those H kids I just hang around with, pretty carefully.

You're right. Then when you choose friendship, you will know that you are making a choice that will stand up—and friends you can stand up for. Friends are special, and special friends are important now that it's time for you to be a teen.

Twenty Fun Things to Do with Close Friends

1. Start a collection. The two of you can spend hours looking for additions to your collection.
2. Share a hobby. Learn a new skill such as cooking, painting, woodworking, playing a musical instrument.
3. Play a sport together. Choose a sport you *both* want to learn. Take lessons if you need them to play really well.
4. Write to a pair of pen pals. To get names, ask your language arts teacher or check a list in a well-known magazine for kids your age. Be sure your moms feel the list you pick your names from is a good one.
5. Begin a contest. Pick a favorite board game. Keep score for two months. At the end of two months, the loser has to take the winner to lunch.
6. Volunteer together at a nursing home or the local animal shelter or _____?
7. Start a book-reading club. Read all the books written by a favorite author. Keep a list as you read them.
8. Make a friendship scrapbook. Paste cutouts and both your writings in it. The two of you write and paste on alternate pages.

9. Walk together three times a week. Start with half a mile each day and work up very slowly to three miles a day. After that, time yourselves and increase your speed. Maybe go out for track after that?

10. Do a Crazy Count. Each of you keeps track of the convertibles you see. (No cheating!) When you get to a hundred, rumor has it that the next person of the opposite sex you meet will have the same first name as the person you will marry someday!

11. Ask one of your dads or moms to let the two of you spend a day at work with them. Find out what they really do.

12. Hold a yard sale. (Get a permit if you need it.) Dig out old clothes, toys, anything your moms say you can get rid of. Tag them. Put out notices. Agree on how to split the money you make. Take down all notices when the sale is over.

13. Organize records and tapes at your house one day and at your friend's house another day.

14. Learn another language together. Get tapes from your library. Talk to each other in the language when you are together.

15. Have an old-fashioned taffy pull. Ask your mom, grandma or uncle to show you how to make it.

16. Have a cooperative pizza party. Ask four friends to bring toppings. You make the crust, your friend makes the sauce. All bring their own drinks.

17. Have a "Sundae" party on Saturday. Furnish the ice

cream and ask friends to bring toppings. You may want to check ahead of time to be sure everyone's favorites will be there.

18. Make up an alphabet code; for example, use z's instead of a's, y's instead of b's, x's instead of c's, etc. Or use numbers or symbols for letters. Send notes using your own private alphabet to each other (but not during class).

19. Be a hugger at the Special Olympics in your area.

20. Cook a joint meal for your families. Pool money. With the help of an adult, decide on a menu. Shop and cook together. When you deliver, add a special touch, like a flower for each table.

What special things do you and your friends like to do? We'd like to know. Write Wirths and Bowman-Kruhm, Box 335, Braddock Heights, MD 21714.

About the Authors

Claudine G. Wirths has a master's degree in psychology and another in special education. She has been a police psychologist and consultant in environmental decision making as well as an educator and member of the adjunct faculty of Frederick (Maryland) Community College. She is now a full-time consultant, speaker, and freelance writer.

Mary Bowman-Kruhm has a doctorate in education. She was a teacher and administrator with Montgomery County (Maryland) Public Schools in regular and special education and has taught at the University of Maryland and Western Maryland College. She is now a full-time freelance writer and consultant/speaker.

Other books by this writing team include *I Hate School! How to Hang In & When to Drop Out* (Harper & Row, 1987), *Where's My Other Sock? How to Get Organized and Drive Your Parents and Teachers Crazy* (Harper & Row, 1989), and *Are You My Type? Or Why Aren't You More Like Me?* (Consulting Psychologists Press, Inc., 1992).

The authors are pleased to be reunited with the illustrator of *I Hate School* on this new project.

photo ©1993 Ruth Lubka

Introducing P. Stren

P. Stren has written and illustrated sixteen books including **I WAS A 15-YEAR-OLD BLIMP, I HATE SCHOOL, FOR SALE: ONE BROTHER** and **HUG ME.** She has created <u>The World of P. Stren</u> and <u>Parlez-Vous Francais?</u>, rubber stamp lines for Rubber Stamps of America. You can find these amazing stamps incorporated into her most recent books.

You can also find her quirky cartoons in her most recent books. Some of her latest cartoons were used by designer Nicole Miller on ties and scarves. (P. Stren admits that she simply *lives* to do cartoons!)

P. Stren is a Canadian. She began her art career in Canada but eventually made her way to New York City where she took the School of Visual Arts by storm! She loved New York so much that she still lives there with her husband, a physician, and their menagerie: a sheltie, an orphan dog from Mexico and a python named Bubba.

54

INDEX

WHEATON